AVENUES
Grammar Review Guide

Lynne Gaetz

Contents

56789   IO I7 I6 I5 I4
34590 ABCD   ENV94

134590

ISBN 978-2-7613-4590-3

IMPRIMÉ AU CANADA
PRINTED IN CANADA

9 782761 345903

ELT

PEARSON   ALWAYS LEARNING

1. Adjectives and Adverbs

Adjectives modify a noun and generally appear before the noun. Adjectives are always singular, even if the nouns they modify are plural.

We admired the **sleek tall** buildings.

Adverbs give information about a verb. Most adverbs end in –*ly*. Some exceptions are the adverbs *fast*, *high*, *far*, *late*, often, and *soon*, which never end in –*ly*.

Liam played the piano **quickly**. (The adverb quickly describes the action of playing.)

COMPARATIVE AND SUPERLATIVE FORMS OF ADJECTIVES AND ADVERBS

		COMPARATIVE	SUPERLATIVE
Add –*er* or –*est* to one-syllable adjectives. When the adjective ends in a consonant-vowel-consonant, double the last letter.	nice young thin	nic**er than** young**er than** thi**nner than**	**the** nic**est** **the** young**est** **the** thi**nnest**
In two-syllable adjectives ending in a consonant + –*y*, change –*y* to –*i* and add –*er* or –*est*.	happy crazy	happ**ier than** craz**ier than**	**the** happ**iest** **the** craz**iest**
Add *more* or *most* to adjectives of two or more syllables and to adverbs ending in –*ly*.	modern slowly	**more** modern **than** **more** slowly **than**	**the most** modern **the most** slowly
Irregular adjectives have special forms.	good / well bad little (small amount) far	**better than** **worse than** **less than** **farther than**	**the best** **the worst** **the least** **the farthest**

EQUALITY: AS ... AS/THE SAME AS

Both *as ... as* and *the same as* express equality.

I am **as tall as** you.   My math mark is **the same as** yours.

FREQUENCY ADVERBS

Adverbs modify verbs and can express time or frequency. Place frequency adverbs

- after *be*   I **am** **often** tired. He **is** **rarely** late.
- before all other simple tense verbs   He **usually** **arrives** on time.
- after an auxiliary verb   She **can** **always** **help** us.
- after the subject in question forms   Does **she** **sometimes** wake up early?

2. Capitalization

Always capitalize
- the pronoun "I" and the first word of every sentence

    The car that **I** drive needs some repairs.

- the days of the week, the months, and holidays

    Wednesday   **S**eptember 8   **L**abour **D**ay

- the names of specific places, such as buildings, streets, parks, public squares, lakes, rivers, cities, provinces, and countries

  Spring **S**treet   Lake **O**ntario   **H**alifax, **N**ova **S**cotia

- the names of languages, nationalities, tribes, races, and religions

  Greek   **M**ohawk   **B**uddhist

- the titles of specific individuals

  General **D**allaire   Prime **M**inister **B**rown   **M**rs. **G**reen

- the titles of specific courses

  Physics 201   **S**panish 100   **B**eginner's **S**panish

- the important words in titles of literary or artistic works

  Source Code   *Modern Family*   *Bad Romance*

3. Combining Sentences

You can combine sentences in a variety of ways.

COORDINATORS AND SUBORDINATORS

Use **coordinators** (*and, but, so, yet*) to connect ideas inside sentences.

  I love the winter, **but** I don't like driving in the snow.

Use **subordinators** (see list below) to connect a secondary idea to a main idea.

  I love the winter **although** I hate cleaning the snow off my car.

COMMON SUBORDINATORS

TIME		REASON, CAUSE, OR EFFECT	CONDITION	CONTRAST	LOCATION
after	when	as	as long as	although	where
before	while	because	if	even though	wherever
since		since	so that	though	
until			unless		

TRANSITIONAL WORDS AND EXPRESSIONS

Use transitional words to connect sentences and paragraphs. When you use the following expressions, put a comma after the expression.

  First, some people drive too fast.

COMMON TRANSITIONAL WORDS AND EXPRESSIONS

CHRONOLOGY (Sequence of ideas)	COMPARISON AND CONTRAST	ADDITIONAL ARGUMENT	EXAMPLE	EMPHASIS	CONCLUDING IDEAS
first, second, third*	however	additionally	for example	above all	finally
later	nevertheless	also	for instance	clearly	in conclusion
next	on the one	as well	in fact	in fact	in short
then	hand	in addition		more	therefore
finally	on the other	furthermore		importantly	thus
suddenly	hand	moreover		of course	to conclude
	similarly			undoubtedly	

* Do not write *firstly, secondly, thirdly*. It is preferable to write *first, second, third*.

4. Determiners

A and *an* mean "one." Only put *a* or *an* before singular count nouns.

- Use *a* before nouns that begin with a consonant.   **a** friend, **a** house

    Exception: When *u* sounds like "you" put a before it.   **a** union

- Use *an* before nouns that begin with a vowel.   **an** apple, **an** umbrella

    Exception: Use *an* before words that begin with a *silent h*.   **an** honest man, **an** hour

Use **the** to indicate a specific noun (or specific nouns). *The* can be placed before singular or plural nouns.

              general   specific

   I need to find **a** new shirt. **The** shirts in that store are expensive.

Note: Do not put *the* before the following:

      sports   languages   the names of most cities, provinces, states, and countries

   I play ~~the~~ hockey. We speak ~~the~~ English. My friend lives in ~~the~~ France.

MUCH, MANY, FEW, AND LITTLE

MANY FEW* / A FEW*	MUCH LITTLE* / A LITTLE*	A LOT OF SOME
Paris has **many** museums.	I have too **much** work.	I took **a lot of** photos.
Very **few** people are there.	I have very **little** time.	Do you have **some** time?
A few museums are closed.	Do you have **a little** money?	

* Notice the differences in meaning. *Few* and *little* mean "almost none." *A few* and *a little* mean "a small amount."
    She has very **few** friends. She has **little** free time. (These are complaints.)
    She has **a few** friends. She has *a* **little** free time. (She is okay with the situation.)

THIS, THAT, THESE, AND THOSE

This and *these* are used to refer to people and things that are close to the speaker. *That* and *those* are used to refer to things that are distant from the speaker.

	NEAR THE SPEAKER	FAR FROM THE SPEAKER
singular	**This** shirt is mine. **This** year I turn twenty-one.	**That** city is in Poland. Remember 1955? My father was born in **that** year.
plural	**These** glasses are mine. **These** days I feel tired.	**Those** cars are driving too fast. I went to school in the 1990s. **Those** years were great.

5. Modals

COMMON MODAL AUXILIARIES			
FUNCTION	MODAL	EXAMPLE	PAST FORM
ability	**can**	She **can speak** English.	**could speak**
polite request	**may** **would** **could** **can**	**May** I **help** you? (formal) **Would** Raul **like** some tea? **Could** you **pass** the butter? **Can** I **help** you? (informal)	

→

advice	**should**	Steve **should stay** with us.	**should have stayed**
	ought to	The doctor **ought to see** her.	**ought to have seen**
obligation	**must**	Jason **must leave** now.	**had to leave**
	have to*	She **has to leave** now.	(past of *must* and *have to*)
probability	**must**	The store **must be** open.	**must have been**
possibility	**could**	Dan **could help** you.	**could have helped**
	might	Mary **might do** the job.	**might have done**
	may	Ann **may help** them.	**may have helped**
condition	**would**	If I had time, I **would help** her. (expresses a wish)	**would have helped**
desire	**would** <u>like</u>	I **would like** some coffee.	**would have liked**
preference	**would** <u>rather</u>	I **would rather be** happy than rich.	**would rather have been**
past habit		In the past, I **would drive** for hours.	

*Although *have to* isn't a modal auxiliary, it is included on this list because it functions like a modal and has the same meaning as *must*. For question and negative forms, you must add *do* or *does*.
> *Does he have to leave? He doesn't have to leave.*

Note: *Gotta* is often heard in spoken English, but it should never be written. It is really an incorrect contraction of *got* and *to*. Make a habit of using *have to* instead of *got to* or *gotta*.

> **have to**
> I ~~gotta~~ find a job.

6. Nouns

A **noun** is a word that refers to a person, place, or thing. A **count noun** refers to a person, place, or thing that can be counted and has a plural form. A **noncount noun** refers to something that cannot be counted and has only a singular form. Often, noncount nouns refer to categories of objects or abstract concepts.

| noncount noun | count noun |
| We had a lot of **homework**. | We have three **assignments**. |

NONCOUNT NOUNS
Here are some common noncount nouns. They have no plural form.

air	clothing	equipment	homework	machinery	pollution	snow
advice	dust	evidence	information	mail	postage	steam
attention	education	furniture	jewellery	makeup	progress	traffic
behaviour	effort	hail	knowledge	mold	proof	violence
change	electricity	health	luck	money	radiation	weather
(money)	energy	help	luggage	music	research	work

Many food items are noncount nouns: bread, coffee, fish, honey, meat, milk, salt, sugar, tea, etc.

PLURAL FORMS
Many English nouns have irregular plural forms.

| man | ▶ | **men** | child | ▶ | **children** | tooth | ▶ | **teeth** | mouse | ▶ | **mice** |
| woman | ▶ | **women** | person | ▶ | **people** | foot | ▶ | **feet** | sheep | ▶ | **sheep** |

Most nouns that end in *–f* or *–fe* change to *–ves* in the plural form. (**Exception:** belief ▶ beliefs)

| shelf | ▶ | **shelves** | life | ▶ | **lives** | scarf | ▶ | **scarves** | thief | ▶ | **thieves** |

7. Phrasal Verbs

Here are some commonly used phrasal verbs.

PHRASAL VERB	MEANING	PHRASAL VERB	MEANING
act up	– to act improperly	find out	– to discover
add up	– to calculate	fool around	– to waste time
back up	– to move in reverse – to support; to make protective copies (computer term)	freak out	– to overreact
blow up	– to explode or inflate	get by	– to survive financially
bone up	– to study	get ready	– to prepare
break down	– to stop working – to collapse emotionally	give away	– to give something for free
break in	– to use force to enter a locked place	give up	– to surrender – to stop a habit (give up alcohol)
break up	– to end a relationship	grow up	– to mature
bring up	– to introduce a subject	hand in	– to submit work to someone
brush up	– to practise	hang out	– to spend time with someone
butt in	– to interrupt	hang up	– to end a phone conversation
butter up	– to praise excessively; flatter	hurry up	– to go faster
call back	– to return a phone call	lay off	– to temporarily dismiss an employee
call off	– to cancel	look after	– to take care of
call up	– to phone someone	make out	– to identify with difficulty – to kiss and touch
carry on	– to continue	make up	– to reunite after a fight
catch on	– to become popular	move over	– to move to the side
check in	– to register at a hotel	pass out	– to distribute – to lose consciousness
chip in	– to contribute	put off	– to postpone
clam up	– to stop talking	rip off	– to steal
close down	– to close permanently	run away	– to secretly leave (home}
close up	– to close temporarily	take after	– to resemble
cross out	– to make an X over something	take back	– to retrieve
cut back	– reduce the use of something	take off	– to remove (clothing) – to leave
dress up	– to wear formal clothing	take over	– to gain control of something
drop off	– to fall asleep – to leave someone or deliver something somewhere – to decline	throw away	– to put in the garbage
drop out	– to quit school	turn off	– to stop a machine or light
figure out	– to solve	turn on	– to start a machine or light
fill in/out	– to complete a form	try on	– wear something to see if it fits

8. Prepositions

IN, ON, AND AT

Use *in*, *on*, and *at* as follows:

In a year, month, city, country, continent

> **In** March, **in** 2012, we stayed **in** London.

On a day of the week, a specific date, a specific street

> **On** March 2, **on** Tuesday, **on** Main Street, we saw a fight.

At a specific time of day, a specific address

> **At** 11:00 **at** night, we stayed **at** a hotel.

FOR AND DURING

Both *for* and *during* indicate that an activity happened over a period of time. However, these words aren't interchangeable. Use *during* to explain when something happened. Use *for* to explain how long it took to happen.

> The restaurant closed **for** two hours **during** the blackout.

> **During** the strike, the hotel workers protested **for** six hours.

PREPOSITIONAL EXPRESSIONS

Many nouns, verbs, and adverbs are usually followed by certain prepositions. Memorize the following prepositional expressions.

afraid (scared) of	depend on	participate in	search for
agree with	insist on	rely on	specialize in
believe in	interested in	responsible for	think about / of

9. Pronouns

A **subject pronoun** performs the action and is usually followed by a verb. An **object pronoun** replaces an object and is usually found after a verb or preposition.

Subject Pronouns:	I	you	he	she	it	we	they
Object Pronouns:	me	you	him	her	it	us	them

She ... **them**

Officer Kate Rowan arrested the bank robbers.

Possessive adjectives describe a noun and appear before the noun that they describe. **Possessive pronouns** replace the possessive adjective and noun.

Possessive Adjectives:	my	your	his	her	its	our	their
Possessive Pronouns:	mine	yours	his	hers	—	ours	theirs

possessive adjective   possessive pronoun

Anne and Rick lost **their** passport.   Did you lose **yours**?

Use **reflexive pronouns** when the subject doing the action and the object receiving the action are the same person or thing.

myself	yourself	himself	herself	itself	ourselves	yourselves	themselves

The small boy dresses **himself**.

HIS, HER, AND ITS

If something belongs to a female, use *her*.	If something belongs to a male, use *his*.	If something belongs to or is part of an object, use *its*.

her brother **her** father **her** house	**his** car **his** mother **his** daughter	**its** muffler **its** wheels **its** seat

TIP

Avoid Pronoun Shifts

A shift occurs when the pronoun doesn't agree with its antecedent. Shifts can also occur within a paragraph.

$$\text{we}$$

We boarded the train. It was so crowded that ~~you~~ couldn't sit down.

10. Punctuation

APOSTROPHES (')

Use apostrophes

- to join a subject and verb together   **We're** late.
- to join an auxiliary with *not*   I **can't** come.
- to indicate possession   **Ross's** computer is new.
    - (plural: add ')   The **girls'** school is closed.
    - (irregular plural: add 's)   The **men's** room is nearby.

COLONS (:)

Use a colon

- after a complete sentence that introduces a list, or after *the following*

    The course has the following sections: crime, law, and justice.

- after a complete sentence that introduces a quotation

    Picasso's advice was clear: "Find your passion."

- to introduce an explanation or example

    I decided to confess: my fingerprints were at the crime scene.

- to separate the hours and minutes in expressions of time

    The store closed at 12:30 and reopened at 2:00.

COMMAS (,)

Use commas

- to separate three or more words in a series (Put the comma before the final *and*.)

    The doctor is tall, thin, and gentle.

- after an introductory word, phrase, or idea

    First, Mr. Chen closed his store.

    A few minutes later, he emptied the safe.

- around interrupting phrases that give additional information about the subject.

    Kevin, a student at Victoria College, went through a traffic light.

PERIODS (.)

Use a period

- at the end of a complete sentence

- after the following titles: *Ms., Mrs., Mr.,* and *Dr.*   (Don't put a period after *Miss*.)

QUOTATION MARKS (" ")

Use quotation marks around direct speech.

Begin a quotation with a capital letter. Put the final comma or period inside the quotation marks.

    He said, **"T**he light was green." **OR** **"T**he light was green," he said.

- Put a comma after an introductory phrase.

    Jacob shouted, **"H**elp me!"

- Put a colon after an introductory sentence.

    The doctor delivered the news: **"Y**ou're healthy."

- When quotations are integrated into sentences, just put quotation marks.

    Dorothy called herself a "terrible mother."

- When a quotation is inside another quotation, use single quotation marks.

    Dante said, "My mother told me, 'Don't be a comedian.'"

SEMICOLONS (;)

Use a semicolon to join two independent and related clauses.

    Gandhi was a pacifist; he believed in non-violence.

11. Spelling

SOME COMMONLY MISSPELLED WORDS

absence	advice (noun)	bargain	career	conscience
accessible	advise (verb)	basically	careful	conscientious
accidentally	alcohol	beginning	changeable	continue
accommodate	another	believe	character	counsellor
accomplish	apartment	benefit	commitment	courteous
accumulate	appearance	between	company	criticism
acquaintance	appointment	business	completely	deceive
address	balloon	calendar	conflict	definitely

→

description	generally	maintenance	personality	responsibility
developed	government	manageable	personal	scientific
discipline	happiness	marriage	(private)	separate
dilemma	height	medicine	personnel (staff)	severely
disappearance	heroes	mentioned	piece	similar
disappoint	historical	millionaire	possess	succeed (verb)
dissatisfied	human	miscellaneous	potato(es)	success (noun)
disease	immediately	mortgage	potential	surely
easily	independence	naturally	practically	statistics
eighth	initiative	necessary	preferred	strength
embarrassed	interesting	necessity	prejudice	technical
encouragement	interrupt	ninety	privilege	technique
environment	jealousy	ninth	proceed	through
exaggerate	judge	noticeable	professor	together
exercise	knowledge	nowadays	proof (noun)	tomorrow
family	language	obstacle	prove (verb)	twelfth
finally	leisure	occasionally	psychology	unique
financially	length	occurred	quantity	usually
forty	lightning	omitted	questioned	writing
fourth	loneliness	organization	questionnaire	
fulfill	loose (not tight)	panicked	really	
function	lose (can't find)	parallel	receive	
future	magazine	permitted	recommend	

12. Verb Tense Review

12.1 PRESENT TENSES

Simple Present	Present Progressive

The **simple present** indicates general truths, facts, and habitual actions.
 	
   Ron **works** every night.
 	
Add –s or –es to verbs that follow third-person singular subjects.
 	
Question: Does he work every night?
Negative: He doesn't work every night.
 	
Keywords: always, often, usually, sometimes, rarely, never, every day, every week …
	The **present progressive** indicates that an action is happening now or for a present, temporary period of time.
	
	   Right now, Ron **is working**.
	
	Question: Is he working?
	Negative: He isn't working.
	
	Keywords: now, at this moment, currently, these days …
	
	Note: Some verbs are non-progressive (see chart on page 12).

Exception: *Be*

Use the verb *be* to identify **age**, **hunger**, **thirst**, **feelings**, **height**, and **temperature**. Remember that the form of the verb must also agree with the subject of the sentence.

I **am** hungry.   Sebastian **is** twenty years old.   They **are** thirsty.

Question and Negative Forms

In questions, just move *be* before the subject. Add *not* to negative forms.

The song is popular.   **Is** the song popular?   The song **is not** popular.

The singers are loud.   **Are** the singers loud?   They **are not** loud.

TIP

Simple Present

- *Have* is irregular. The third-person singular form is *has*.   Judy **has** three children.
- *Everybody* is considered third-person singular.   Everybody **likes** coffee.
- There **is** <u>one thing</u>. There **are** <u>two or more things</u>.

12.2 PAST TENSES

Simple Past	Past Progressive
The **simple past** indicates that an action was completed at an understood past time. 　Last night, he **watched** TV. **Question:** Did he watch TV? **Negative:** He didn't watch TV. **Keywords:** ago, yesterday, last week, when I was young, many years ago …	The **past progressive** indicates that an action was in progress at a specific past time or when another action interrupted it. 　Last night, he **was watching** TV when I called. **Question:** Was he watching TV when …? **Negative:** He wasn't watching TV when …. **Keywords:** while, during …

EXCEPTION: *BE*

There are two past forms of the verb *be*. To form questions, simply move *was* or *were* before the subject. Just add *not* to negative forms.

- **I/He/She/It was:**   She **was** nice. **Was** the job difficult? It **wasn't** hard.
- **You/We/They were:**   You **were** tired. **Were** they late? They **weren't** late.

TIP

Past Tenses

- **Simple Past** – In question and negative forms, use the base form of the verb.

　　　　　help
　Did she ~~helped~~ you?

- **Past Progressive** – Do not use the past progressive to talk about past habits or about a series of past actions. Only use this tense to emphasize that an action was in progress.

NON-PROGRESSIVE VERBS

The following verbs are generally not used in the progressive tense.

PERCEPTION	PREFERENCE	MENTAL STATE/OPINION	POSSESSION
appear & seem	dislike	believe	belong
feel	hate	forget	have (meaning "possess")
hear	like	know	own
resemble	love	mean	possess
see	need	recognize	
smell	prefer	remember	
sound	want	think (meaning "in my opinion")	
taste		understand	

12.3 FUTURE TENSES

The future tenses indicate that an action will occur at a future time. You can use *will* or *be going to* plus the verb.

WILL	*(BE) GOING TO*

Will + verb indicates a future action. Also indicates a spontaneous or voluntary decision.
 	
    He **will help** you.
 	
Question: Will he help you?
Negative: He won't help you.
	(Be) going to + verb indicates a future action and a definite future plan.
	
	    Next week, they **are going to do** the job.
	
	Question: Are they going to do the job?
	Negative: They aren't going to do the job.

Keywords: soon, later, tomorrow, the day after tomorrow, next week, next month, in five years ...	

TIME CLAUSES

In sentences that indicate the future, use the present tense in time clauses. A time clause begins with a **time marker** such as *when*. Never use the future tense after these time markers:

after   before   until
as soon as   unless   when/whenever

time marker
    When I **finish** college, I **will try to find** an interesting job.

PRESENT TENSES

Present tenses can indicate future actions.

- The present progressive can refer to a previously planned event.

    Next December, we **are visiting** Mexico.

- The simple present can be used to talk about schedules and timetables.

    The train **leaves** at midnight.   The football game **starts** at 2 p.m. tomorrow.

THE FUTURE PROGRESSIVE

The future progressive indicates that an action *will be* in progress at a future time. The tense is formed with *will be* + an "ing" verb.

    Tomorrow, when you come to my office, I **will be working**.

Use *Going To*, Not "Gonna"

Gonna is *not* a proper word. Instead, use *going to*.

> **going to**
> Miranda is ~~gonna~~ call you.

12.4 PRESENT PERFECT TENSES

PRESENT PERFECT

The **present perfect** can be used in two distinct ways:

1) when an action began in the past and continues to the present.

    Keywords: since, for, ever, not … yet, so far, up to now

Simon **has lived** alone since 1996.
(The event began in 1996 and continues to the present.)

2) when the time of a past action (or past actions) is not important or not specified.

    Keywords: already, once, twice, several times, many times (before now)

Simon **has visited** Italy many times.
(The visits occurred at unspecified past times.)

PRESENT PERFECT PROGRESSIVE

The **present perfect progressive** is used to indicate that an action has been in progress (without interruption) from a past time up to the present. This tense emphasizes the duration of an activity.

> Mark **has been reading** for six hours.

Since* vs. *For

- ***Since*** refers to a specific time in the past when the action began (since I graduated, since I was a child, since 1995, etc.).
- ***For*** refers to the amount of time that the action lasted (for six months, for years, for a few hours, etc.).

Present Perfect

Do not use the present perfect tense when the past time is known.

> **visited**
> Two years ago, we ~~have visited~~ Florida.

12.5 PAST PERFECT TENSE

The **past perfect** tense indicates that one past action happened before another past action. It is formed with *had* + the past participle.

Keywords: up to that time, already

Last night, the robbers **had** already **left** when the police arrived at the bank.

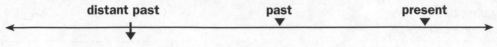

| distant past | past | present |

The robbers **had left** when the police arrived.

13. Questions

Yes/No questions begin with an auxiliary. The answer to these questions is "yes" or "no."

Do you live in an apartment?   <u>Yes</u>, I do.   <u>No</u>, I don't.

Information questions begin with question words, such as *who, what, when, where, why, how*, etc.

<u>When</u> did you move here?   <u>How often</u> do you travel?

Subject questions ask about the subject. When *who, what,* and *how many* ask about the <u>subject</u> of a question, no auxiliary is needed.

Who needs to borrow some money?   **What** looks beautiful?

Alex needs to borrow some money.   **His house** looks beautiful.

QUESTION STRUCTURE

Questions have the following word order.

QUESTION WORD	AUXILIARY	SUBJECT	VERB	REST OF SENTENCE
	Do	you	want	to eat?
	Does	she	work?	
What	**are**	you	doing?	
Why	**did**	Mark	leave	yesterday?
When	**should**	we	visit	you?

QUESTION WORDS

QUESTION WORD	REFERS TO	QUESTION WORD	REFERS TO
Who	**a person** **Who** are you? **Who** do you work with?	How	**a method or degree** **How** did you make this? **How** cold is it?
What	**a thing** **What** is your name?	How long	**a period of time** **How long** is the movie?
When	**a time** **When** does the show start?	How far	**a distance** **How far** is Laval from here?
Where	**a place** **Where** do you live?	How often	**the frequency of an activity** **How often** do you see a dentist?
Why	**a reason** **Why** is he late?	How much/ How many	**an amount of something** **How much** does it cost? **How many** people are there?
Which	**a choice** **Which** salad do you want?	How old	**age** **How old** is Lucas?

QUESTIONS IN ALL VERB TENSES

SIMPLE PRESENT

Do — I / you / we / they — work?
Does — he / she / it — work?

SIMPLE PAST

Did — I / he / she / it / you / we / they — walk?

PRESENT PROGRESSIVE

Am — I — working?
Is — he / she / it / you — working?
Are — we / they — working?

PAST PROGRESSIVE

Was — I / he / she / it — working?
Were — you / we / they — working?

FUTURE—WILL

Will — I / he / she / it / you / we / they — try?

MODALS

Can — I / he / she / it / you / we / they — swim?

Be

PRESENT

Am — I — busy?
Is — he / she / it / you — busy?
Are — we / they — busy?

PAST

Was — I / he / she / it — ready?
Were — you / we / they — ready?

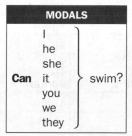

14. Common Irregular Verbs

BASE FORM	SIMPLE PAST	PAST PARTICIPLE	BASE FORM	SIMPLE PAST	PAST PARTICIPLE
be	was/were	been	draw	drew	drawn
beat	beat	beat/beaten	drink	drank	drunk
become	became	become	drive	drove	driven
begin	began	begun	eat	ate	eaten
bend	bent	bent	fall	fell	fallen
bet	bet	bet	feed	fed	fed
bite	bit	bitten	feel	felt	felt
bleed	bled	bled	fight	fought	fought
blow	blew	blown	find	found	found
break	broke	broken	fit	fit	fit
bring	brought	brought	fly	flew	flown
build	built	built	forbid	forbade	forbidden
buy	bought	bought	forget	forgot	forgotten
catch	caught	caught	forgive	forgave	forgiven
choose	chose	chosen	freeze	froze	frozen
come	came	come	get	got	got/gotten
cost	cost	cost	give	gave	given
cut	cut	cut	go	went	gone
deal	dealt	dealt	grow	grew	grown
dig	dug	dug	hang[1]	hung	hung
do	did	done	have	had	had

1. When *hang* means "to suspend by a rope, as in a form of capital punishment," then it is a regular verb. The past forms are *hanged*.

hear	heard	heard	**shrink**	shrank	shrunk
hide	hid	hidden	**shut**	shut	shut
hit	hit	hit	**sing**	sang	sung
hold	held	held	**sink**	sank	sunk
hurt	hurt	hurt	**sit**	sat	sat
keep	kept	kept	**sleep**	slept	slept
know	knew	known	**slide**	slid	slid
lay[2]	laid	laid	**speak**	spoke	spoken
lead	led	led	**speed**	sped	sped
leave	left	left	**spend**	spent	spent
lend	lent	lent	**spin**	spun	spun
let	let	let	**split**	split	split
lie[3]	lay	lain	**spread**	spread	spread
light	lit	lit	**stand**	stood	stood
lose	lost	lost	**steal**	stole	stolen
make	made	made	**stick**	stuck	stuck
mean	meant	meant	**sting**	stung	stung
meet	met	met	**stink**	stank	stunk
mistake	mistook	mistaken	**strike**	struck	struck
pay	paid	paid	**swear**	swore	sworn
put	put	put	**sweep**	swept	swept
prove	proved	proved/proven	**swim**	swam	swum
quit	quit	quit	**swing**	swung	swung
read[4]	read	read	**take**	took	taken
ride	rode	ridden	**teach**	taught	taught
ring	rang	rung	**tear**	tore	torn
rise	rose	risen	**tell**	told	told
run	ran	run	**think**	thought	thought
say	said	said	**throw**	threw	thrown
see	saw	seen	**understand**	understood	understood
sell	sold	sold	**upset**	upset	upset
send	sent	sent	**wake**	woke	woken
set	set	set	**wear**	wore	worn
shake	shook	shaken	**win**	won	won
shoot	shot	shot	**withdraw**	withdrew	withdrawn
show	showed	shown	**write**	wrote	written

2. *Lay* means "to set or place something on a surface." It is always followed by a noun. Example: I laid my book on the desk.
3. *Lie* means "to rest or lie down, such as on a sofa or bed." When *lie* means "to tell a false statement," it is a regular verb: *lie–lied–lied*.
4. The present form of *read* is pronounced "reed." The simple past and past participle forms are pronounced "red."